SING-ALONG SOUL
WITH A LIVE BAND!

WISE PUBLICATIONS
part of The Music Sales Group
London / New York / Paris / Sydney / Copenhagen / Berlin / Madrid / Tokyo

Published by
WISE PUBLICATIONS
14-15 Berners Street, London W1T 3LJ, UK.

Exclusive Distributors:
MUSIC SALES LIMITED
Distribution Centre, Newmarket Road, Bury St Edmunds, Suffolk IP33 3YB, UK.
MUSIC SALES PTY LIMITED
20 Resolution Drive, Caringbah, NSW 2229, Australia.

Order No. AM999020
ISBN 978-1-84938-310-3
This book © Copyright 2009 Wise Publications, a division of Music Sales Limited.

Compiled by Nick Crispin
Edited by Lizzie Moore
Series Editor: Fiona Bolton
Music arranged by Paul Honey
Music processed by Paul Ewers Music Design
Song Background Notes by Michael Heatley
Cover design by Adela Casacuberta
Text photographs courtesy LFI
Printed in the EU

CD recorded, mixed and mastered by Jonas Persson
Keyboard: Paul Honey
Guitar: Arthur Dick
Bass: Don Richardson
Drums: Chris Baron
Vocals: Rikki Ancell and Kirsten Joy Gill

YOUR GUARANTEE OF QUALITY
As publishers, we strive to produce every book to the highest commercial standards.
This book has been carefully designed to minimise awkward page turns and to make playing
from it a real pleasure.
Particular care has been given to specifying acid-free, neutral-sized paper made from
pulps which have not been elemental chlorine bleached. This pulp is from farmed
sustainable forests and was produced with special regard for the environment.
Throughout, the printing and binding have been planned to ensure a sturdy, attractive
publication which should give years of enjoyment.
If your copy fails to meet our high standards, please inform us and we will gladly replace it.

www.musicsales.com

FREE bonus material

Download band scores and parts to your computer.

Visit www.hybridpublications.com

Registration is free and easy.

Your registration code is: AS546

Song Background Notes

Cry To Me
Solomon Burke

The gospel fervour of this offering from Philadelphia-born Solomon Burke caught the ear of many on its release, and was perhaps not surprising bearing in mind he started out as a preacher before turning to secular soul. The Pretty Things and The Rolling Stones have both made cover versions of the song, but it was in 1987, when used in the film *Dirty Dancing*, in the famous scene in which Baby and Johnny seduce each other whilst dancing, that another generation awoke to the song's power. Mary J. Blige inducted Burke into the Rock And Roll Hall of Fame in 2001.

I Get The Sweetest Feeling
Jackie Wilson

Three times a hit in Britain, this feel-good track from soul legend Jackie Wilson was a US hit in the late 1960s. It started life as a Motown song co-written by Van McCoy (of 'The Hustle' fame) and Alicia Evelyn, but quickly became Wilson's own with help from orchestrator Willie Henderson. After the chart-topping success of the Claymation video-led re-release of 'Reet Petite' in 1986, two years after Wilson's death, this track was also re-released and peaked at No.3 in the UK Chart. The song was used in the movie *High Fidelity*, and cover versions have been recorded by Will Young and Atomic Kitten Liz McClarnon.

I Got You (I Feel Good)
James Brown

Good things come to those who wait. Godfather of soul James Brown originally wrote this song in 1962 for one of his backing singers, Yvonne Fair, but liked it so much he kept it for himself. He took it into the studio in 1964, but a record label dispute held up release. Undaunted, he recorded it again in 1965 and it became the first of many gold records to emerge from Criteria Studios in Miami where *Saturday Night Fever* would later be created. James Brown's signature song, it contains many of his musical trademarks including horn riffs, tempo changes and hollers.

In The Midnight Hour
Wilson Pickett

After an initial hitless year as a recording artist, time was running out for Wilson Pickett, but he stopped the clock in 1965 with this track. Producer Jerry Wexler sent the singer to the hot music city of Memphis, where he wrote this song (and later many other hits) with guitarist Steve Cropper of Booker T & the MG's. The rhythm was designed to suit a then-current dance craze, 'the jerk'. Roxy Music would give the song an unlikely glam-pop makeover when they re-formed in the late 1970s, reflecting ex-soulboy Bryan Ferry's youthful listening habits.

Knock On Wood
Eddie Floyd

The similarity between Eddie Floyd's biggest hit 'Knock On Wood' and Wilson Pickett's 'In The Midnight Hour' may have stemmed from co-writer Steve Cropper, who assisted both singers, and stopped the former being released until 1966, the year after 'In The Midnight Hour' made it into the charts. 'Knock On Wood' was written on a stormy night, hence the lyrical reference to thunder and lightning, and may well have been intended for Otis Redding, whose belated duet version of the song with Carla Thomas emerged in 1967. The song was also covered successfully by disco diva Amii Stewart (UK No.6, 1979) and David Bowie (UK No.10, 1974).

Son Of A Preacher Man
Dusty Springfield

The success of the album *Dusty In Memphis*, of which this was the killer cut, underlined the fact that soul comes from within and is not determined by skin colour. The former Mary O'Brien had travelled to the Stax studios in 1968 and was offered the song only after Aretha Franklin turned it down. By the time Lady Soul reconsidered, Dusty's version had become definitive. A transatlantic Top 10 entry in early 1969, this would be Dusty Springfield's last hit for 20 years. The song has been covered by innumerable female singers but it was the original that featured in the 1994 film *Pulp Fiction*.

Soul Man
Sam & Dave

Among the intros of Stax Records' many memorable hits, the guitar lick that introduces 'Soul Man', played by ace guitarist Steve Cropper, is the most recognisable. The song proved to be the career peak of Sam (Moore) and Dave (Prater), who, after its No.2 US pop success in 1967, found their relationship and career on the skids. The song itself however, written by Isaac Hayes and David Porter and based on the famous 'Bo Diddley' rhythm, was revived for the big screen over a decade later by the Blues Brothers. Its lyrics also made it an anthem for the black consciousness and black pride movements, the concept of soul linked with self-worth and community.

Stand By Me
Ben E. King

This song was only Ben E. King's second solo release after leaving the Drifters in 1960. Twenty-seven years later it topped the UK chart and revived his by-then waning career. It was boosted by use as the title song of a Stephen King horror movie, but the inspiration of the song had been the gospel group once fronted by Sam Cooke. 'I took it from a spiritual the Soul Stirrers did,' said King, co-writer with producers Jerry Leiber and Mike Stoller. Someone else who had listened to the original release was John Lennon, who covered it on his 1975 collection of classic oldies, *Rock And Roll,* turning it into a hit of his own.

Tired Of Being Alone
Al Green

Al Green, or the Reverend Al Green as he now is, brought a gospel purity to the soul world, assisted by Memphis producer Willie Dixon who would go on to be employed by Wet Wet Wet and others in later years. They may have sought his magic, but it was Green alone who had the voice. Written in late 1968, it proved problematical to record and as such took until 1971 to become his first US Top 40 hit. A signature track since appearing on *Al Green Gets Next To You*, the song featured in the movie *Dead Presidents*, in which Green is seen singing on a TV set.

Try A Little Tenderness
Otis Redding

Written by Irving King (a pseudonym used by the song-writing duo James Campbell and Reginald Connelly) and Harry M. Woods, this song dates back to 1933 and crooner Bing Crosby. Aretha Franklin was the first to record it soul-style in 1962, but all subsequent performances by the likes of Rod Stewart and Tina Turner have referenced Otis Redding's definitive 1966 version which progresses from balladic beginning to stomping climax in three and a half minutes. The only version Otis knew, by idol and mentor, Sam Cooke, featured just two verses as it was part of a live medley, so he performed it that way too. The song was brought to a new generation on the big screen in 1991 by *The Commitments*.

Ben E. King

James Brown

Dusty Springfield

Otis Redding

Sam & Dave

Wilson Pickett

Cry To Me

Words & Music by Bert Russell

Demo track: Track 01
Backing track: Track 11

Steadily ♩ = 114

I Get The Sweetest Feeling

Words & Music by Van McCoy & Alicia Evelyn

Demo track: Track 02
Backing track: Track 12

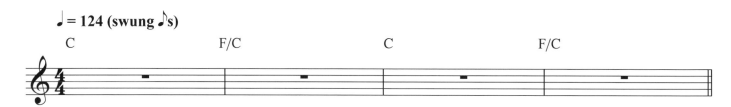

1. The clos-er you get,____ the bet-ter you look,____ ba - by.____
2. The warm-er your kiss,____ the deep-er you touch____ me,____ ba - by.

The bet-ter you look,____ the more____ I want you.____
The deep-er your touch,____ the more____ you thrill me.

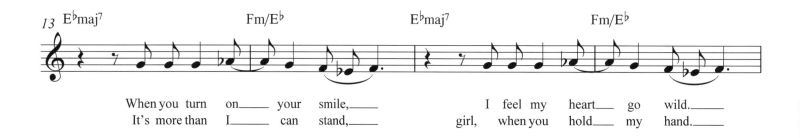

When you turn on____ your smile,____ I feel my heart____ go wild.____
It's more than I____ can stand,____ girl, when you hold____ my hand.

I'm__ like a child____ with a brand new toy.____ And I get the
I feel so__ grand____ that I could cry.____ And I get the

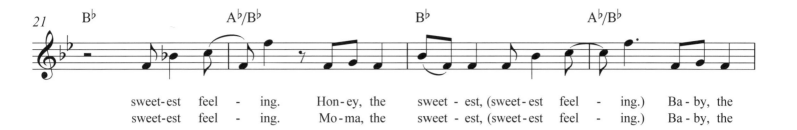

sweet-est feel - ing. Hon-ey, the sweet - est, (sweet-est feel - ing.) Ba - by, the
sweet-est feel - ing. Mo - ma, the sweet - est, (sweet-est feel - ing.) Ba - by, the

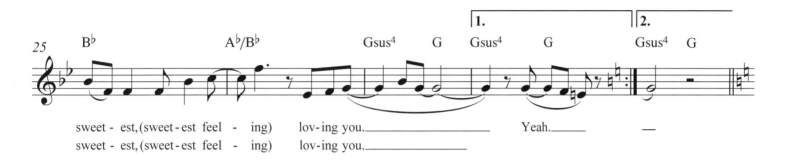

sweet - est,(sweet-est feel - ing) lov-ing you._____ Yeah.___ —
sweet - est,(sweet-est feel - ing) lov-ing you._____

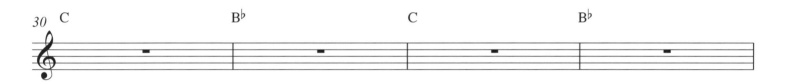

3. The great-er your love,___ the strong-er you hold___ me,___ ba - by.

The strong-er your hold,___ the more___ I need you._____

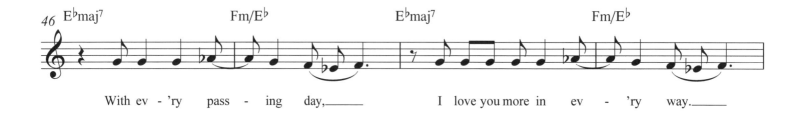

With ev - 'ry pass - ing day,_____ I love you more in ev - 'ry way._____

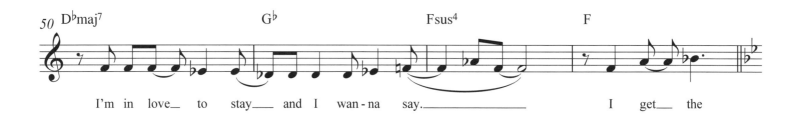

I'm in love_ to stay_ and I wan - na say._____ I get_ the

(sweet - est feel - ing.) Ba - by, the sweet - est, (sweet - est feel - ing.) Hon - ey, the

sweet - est, (sweet - est feel - ing.) Lov - ing you._____

(Sweet - est feel - ing.) Ba - by, the sweet - est, (sweet - est feel - ing.) Ba - by, the sweet - est, (sweet - est feel -

- ing.) Ba - by the sweet - est, (sweet - est feel - ing.) Lov - ing you.

In The Midnight Hour

Words & Music by Wilson Pickett & Steve Cropper

Demo track: Track 03
Backing track: Track 13

I Got You (I Feel Good)

Words & Music by James Brown

Demo track: Track 04
Backing track: Track 14

Moderate rock feel ♩ = 140

Knock On Wood

Words & Music by Steve Cropper & Eddie Floyd

Demo track: Track 05
Backing track: Track 15

Son Of A Preacher Man

Words & Music by John Hurley & Ronnie Wilkins

Demo track: Track 06
Backing track: Track 16

looking to see___ how much_ we'd grown. And the on - ly one___ who could ev - er reach_ me,

was the son of a preach-er man.___ The on - ly boy___ who could ev - er teach_ me,

was the son of a preach - er man. Yes, he was, he was.

Oh, yes, he was.___ The on - ly one___ who could ev - er reach_ me,

was the son of a preach-er man. The on - ly boy___ who could ev - er teach_ me,

was the son of a preach-er man. The on - ly one___ who could ev - er woo_ me,

was the son of a preach-er man. The on - ly one___ who could ev - er woo_ me,

was the son of a preach - er man. He was, he was.

Oh, yes, he was.___

Soul Man

Words & Music by Isaac Hayes & David Porter

Demo track: Track 07
Backing track: Track 17

Stand By Me

Words & Music by Ben E. King, Jerry Leiber & Mike Stoller

Demo track: Track 08
Backing track: Track 18

Tired Of Being Alone

Words & Music by Al Green

Demo track: Track 09
Backing track: Track 19

in my dreams_____ no-bod - y but you, ba - by. Some-times I won-der,

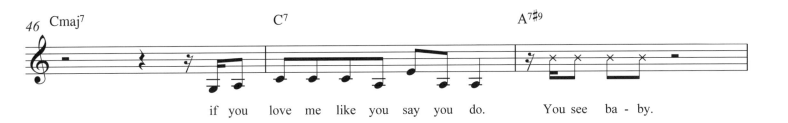

if you love me like you say you do. You see ba - by.

Need-ing you has pro - ven to me_____ to be my___ great - est dream, yeah._

___ I'm so tired_____ of be - in' a - lone, so tired___ of be - in' a - lone, so tired_

___ of be - in' a - lone._____ I'm so tired_____ of be - in' a - lone, so tired_

___ of be - in' a - lone, so tired___ of be - in' a - lone._____

Try A Little Tenderness

Words & Music by Harry Woods, Jimmy Campbell & Reg Connelly

Demo track: Track 10
Backing track: Track 20

Squeeze____ her, don't tease____ her, nev - er leave her, get to her. Just,

just, just try a lit - tle ten - der - ness, yeah, yeah, yeah.____ You got - ta, know how to

love her, man.____ Take this ad - vice, man,____ you got to squeeze____ her, don't tease____ her.

Nev - er leave,____ you got - ta hold her, and, broth - er, some-thing else, try a lit - tle

tend - er - ness, yeah, yeah, yeah.____ You got - ta, know how to love her, man.____

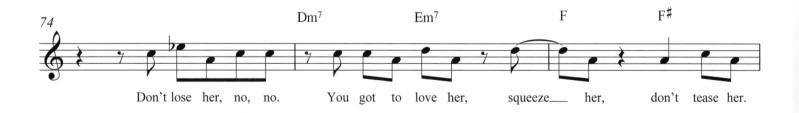

Don't lose her, no, no. You got to love her, squeeze____ her, don't tease her.

rall.

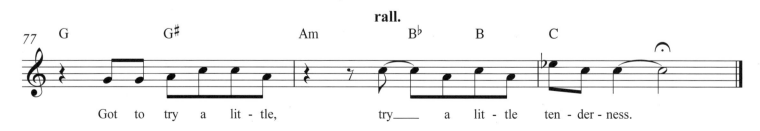

Got to try a lit - tle, try____ a lit - tle ten - der - ness.

123456789